EVERYDAY MADE EASY

APPLE iOS & iPHONE BASICS

This is a **FLAME TREE** book
First published 2015

Publisher and Creative Director: Nick Wells
Project Editor: Polly Prior
Art Director and Layout Design: Mike Spender
Digital Design and Production: Chris Herbert
Copy Editor: Anna Groves
Proofreader: Dawn Laker
Indexer: Helen Snaith
Screenshots: Chris Smith

Special thanks to: Laura Bulbeck, Josie Mitchell

This edition first published 2015 by
FLAME TREE PUBLISHING
Crabtree Hall, Crabtree Lane
Fulham, London SW6 6TY
United Kingdom

www.flametreepublishing.com

15 17 19 18 16
1 3 5 7 9 10 8 6 4 2

© 2015 Flame Tree Publishing

ISBN 978-1-78361-394-6

A CIP record for this book is available from the British Library upon request.

Printed in China

All non-screenshot pictures are courtesy of © 2015 Apple Inc.: 77b; and Shutterstock and © the following photographers: 1 charnsitr; 2,
3, 6, 7, 8, 81, 85, 116 Denys Prykhodov; 5, 64, 92, 109, 122 Twin Design; 12l Jon Le-Bon; 12c, 32, 84 Bloomua; 12r Ekaterina_Minaeva;
13l, 17 & 78 Ingvar Bjork; 13r, 34b, 35tl, 35tr, 35b Oleg GawriloFF; 15c Kostsov; 15t, 15b NorGal; 26, 51 blvdone; 31, 102 Kaspars
Grinvalds; 34t, 90 Zeynep Demir; 42 Goran Bogicevic; 54 EurngKwan; 55 Peter Bernik; 56 rzoze19; 60, 61, 118, 125 Hadrian; 69 Olga
Lebedeva; 71 Natalia Kirichenko; 73 KieferPix; 75 Olesya Kuznetsova; 77t Oleksandr Chub; 94 BigLike Images; 98 Linda Moon; 101 Nina
Buday; 104 nemke; 108 Syda Productions; 110 Lichtmeister; 112 Neirfy.

EVERYDAY GUIDES
MADE EASY

APPLE iOS
& iPHONE
BASICS

CHRIS SMITH

**FLAME TREE
PUBLISHING**

CONTENTS

Set up your iPhone for the first time and find your way around the iOS operating system.

Familiarize yourself with the features on your new phone, import your contacts,
make calls and send texts.

Log on to the internet to browse the web, set up your email accounts,
meet Siri and master Maps.

Learn about the built-in apps on your iPhone and how to download new ones
from the App Store.

Take photos and videos and share them, while discovering how
to get the best music, videos and games on your device.

Overcome common issues, conserve memory and battery life, and learn
to protect your iPhone's most precious data.

SERIES FOREWORD

Since Apple launched the iPhone in 2007, and followed it up with the iPad in 2010, the consumer touchscreen technology sector has increased exponentially. There is now a bewildering variety of choices to make about the smartphone and tablet devices we carry with us, but this Apple iOS & iPhone Basics guide is here to help you navigate many of them.

Whether you're looking for entertainment, music, social connectivity, any business service you can think of, or a source of information about where you are and what you're looking at that very second, this Apple iOS & iPhone Basics guide will help you navigate the world of touchscreen tech and apps.

As with other titles in this series, we take a detailed look at the iPhone, how to set it up and get the best out of it for your lifestyle, as well as how to get to grips with the basics of iOS, Apple's operating system. Don't worry, though – this guide is designed for absolute beginners, as well as those who are looking for more expert knowledge.

Finally, there's a comprehensive troubleshooting guide, full of the best tips and tricks to keep you and your device and operating system working in perfect harmony. Throughout each chapter there are Hot Tips to save you time and effort – keep a sharp look out!

This easy-to-use, step-by-step guide is written by a recognized expert in his field, so you can be sure of the best advice and the latest knowledge without breaking a sweat. The Apple iOS & iPhone Basics guide is an asset to any reference bookshelf – happy reading.

Mark Mayne
Editor of T3.com

INTRODUCTION

Welcome to the exciting new world of Apple iPhone. With this miraculous, pocket-size device in the palm of your hand, you'll soon be snapping and sharing great photos, browsing the internet, keeping up with your family via email, watching movies, finding directions, streaming music, posting to Facebook, playing addictive games and so much more. Oh, and did we mention you can make calls and send texts too?

A SIMPLE SYSTEM

The key to unlocking all this potential is the iOS operating system, the simple and straightforward touch-based software that powers every Apple iPhone. This book will break down the basics of using iOS, from setting up for the first time and finding your way around, all the way through to some of the more complex tasks, such as taking, editing and sharing a photograph.

STEP-BY-STEP GUIDES

In easily digestible steps, you'll learn to set up all of your internet accounts, master built-in applications and download new and exciting experiences via the App Store. You'll even learn how to quickly solve the common issues that have frustrated iPhone users in the past.

OLDER VERSIONS

The vast majority of iPhones run either iOS 7 or iOS 8. Only around four per cent of iPhones use iOS 6 or older. This book will focus on iOS 8, but also references any differences to iOS 7.

PRO ADVICE

This book is loaded with helpful screenshots, and look out too for the handy Hot Tips scattered throughout the next six chapters. We don't expect you to read this book cover to cover, but we hope it will be a great reference point as and when you need a little help on your iOS journey. Enjoy!

GETTING STARTED

WHAT IS APPLE iOS?

Every iPhone, iPad and iPod comes fitted with software called iOS. The operating system allows users to answer phone calls, browse the internet, play video games, take photos, get directions and underpins every feature on the iPhone.

USING iOS

iOS is a touchscreen-based operating system. It is controlled by tapping the screen to open apps, select music tracks, type messages on a virtual keyboard and perform many other functions. Users can also find their way around by means of a variety of gestures like swipes, scrolls, pinches, double taps and more.

The Evolution of iOS

Apple regularly updates and improves iOS, often more than once per year. Updated versions bring new features, while enhancing existing ones. The latest version, iOS 8, was released with the iPhone 6 and iPhone 6 Plus in 2014.

Left: The iOS 8 homescreen.

iOS 8 FEATURES

Here are some of the new features you can enjoy with iOS 8.

- **Message app**: Use this app to send live video and audio messages.

- **Enhanced keyboard**: An enhanced keyboard with smart word predictions.

- **Family sharing**: Family sharing enables the use of one credit card for all of your family's accounts.

- **New design details**: New design details, including displaying your favourite contacts in the multitasking view.

Older Versions

The vast majority of iPhones run either iOS 7 or iOS 8. Only around four per cent of iPhones use iOS 6 or older. This book will focus on iOS 8, but we'll point out any differences to iOS 7.

Below: The new multitasking view in iOS 8.

Hot Tip

You don't need the latest iPhone to run iOS 8. Updating to the latest version is easy for all iPhones released since 2011. *See* page 124.

WHAT IS AN iPHONE?

The iPhone is a mobile phone – often called a smartphone – made by Apple and running iOS. It is designed to be a communications tool, compact camera, gaming machine, media player and a personal computer all in one palm-size device.

DIFFERENT VERSIONS

The latest handsets are 2014's iPhone 6 (4.7-inch) and the iPhone 6 Plus (5.5-inch), which have a revamped, slimmer design. Here are some of the devices still widely available new or second hand.

Hot Tip

All of the iPhones listed can be updated to iOS 8. Head to Settings > General > Software Update to get started (*see* page 124 for more info).

Above: The iPhone 4S.

Above: The iPhone 5C.

- **iPhone 4S (2011)**: 3.5-inch screen, of square, metallic design.

- **iPhone 5 (2012)**: First Apple handset with a 4-inch screen.

- **iPhone 5C (2013)**: A cheaper and more colourful version of the iPhone 5.

- **iPhone 5S (2013)**: 4-inch screen with a Touch ID fingerprint sensor.

- **iPhone 6 and 6 Plus (2014)**: The iPhone 6 has a 4.7-inch screen, while the 6 Plus has a 5.5-inch screen. But while the displays are larger than before, the phones are also thinner.

Above: The iPhone 5S.

Above: The iPhone 5.

Above: The iPhone 6 and 6 Plus.

THE BENEFITS OF AN iPHONE

If you've acquired an iPhone, there are endless benefits you can now enjoy with your new handset. Here are some of them.

- **Calls and texts**: It's still a phone, after all!

- **Internet**: Follow your favourite sites through Safari.

- **Photos**: Take snaps and videos and share them online.

- **Email**: Compose, send, read and reply.

- **Games**: Download a host of fun and challenging games from the App Store.

- **Media**: Listen to music and watch movies and TV shows.

- **Books**: Use your iPhone as an e-book reader.

- **Maps**: Get from A to B easily, thanks to the built-in compass and GPS sensor.

Below: Apple Maps can serve as an alternative to using a satnav.

- **Apps**: The App Store features endless tools to enhance your iPhone experience.

GETTING STARTED WITH iOS

Before you can begin embracing this exciting new mobile world, we'll need to take a few steps to get the device set up.

PREPARING FOR SET-UP

Make sure you have a working SIM card and an active account with a mobile network, such as O2, Vodafone, EE or Three. If you're buying the iPhone new, this will all be taken care of.

Inserting the SIM and Charging

Insert the SIM card (face down) into the pop-out tray on the side of the device (the iPhone comes with a neat tool for opening the tray). If you're buying an iPhone in person, a store assistant will be happy to help. Finally, it's advisable to charge your phone for an hour or so before switching on.

Hot Tip
Make sure you have the right size SIM card. The iPhone 5, 5C, 5S, 6 and 6 Plus all use the tiny NanoSIM standard.

Above: The NanoSIM is much smaller than a normal SIM card, but holds just as much data.

POWERING UP YOUR iPHONE

Simply hold down the iPhone's power button for a second. You'll soon be greeted with a white Apple icon, which means you're underway.

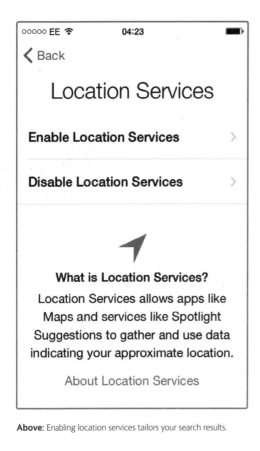

Above: Enabling location services tailors your search results.

iPhone and iOS Set-up

Once power-up has completed, you'll see a welcome screen. Swipe right to enter the Set-Up Assistant and tap the touchscreen to make selections.

- **Choose your language and region:** This will affect time zones, keyboards and app store regions.

- **Choose a Wi-Fi network:** Choose your home network (the network name is on the router) and enter your password via the on-screen keyboard.

- **Enable location services:** This will allow you to use maps and search for location-specific information such as nearby restaurants. This can be toggled later.

SETTING UP A NEW iPHONE

If you've never used an iPhone before, choose 'Set up as new iPhone'. We'll deal with restoring later in the book.

Apple ID

An Apple ID allows you to download apps, purchase media content, synchronize your accounts and much more. If you have an Apple ID, insert the username and password here. If not, you can easily set up a free account.

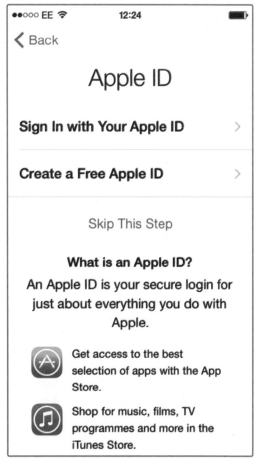

1. Insert your birthday as a means of retrieving your password.

2. Enter your name and email address (or set up an @icloud.com account there and then) and then choose a password.

3. Answer and memorize some security questions.

4. Select a 'rescue email address' if you wish (this will help if you forget your password) and opt in or out of Apple marketing emails.

5. Agree to Apple's terms and conditions.

Above: Setting up an Apple ID allows you to buy apps, games and more.

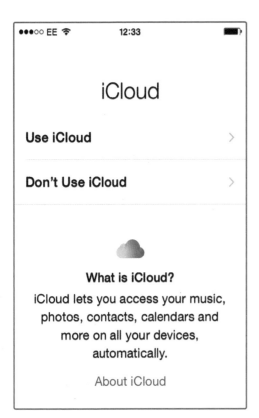

Hot Tip

iCloud is great for backing up your important data, but there have been recent security worries, with personal photos leaked online. If you're uncomfortable about this, you can decline to use iCloud.

iCloud

An iCloud account safeguards your photos, data, app purchases and more. You'll be asked to upgrade to iCloud Drive (iOS 8 only), which allows you to store more files and access them on other iOS devices or Mac computers. We'll skip this step for now.

Enable Find My iPhone

This facility can be used to track the last-known whereabouts of your iPhone or to wipe contents via iCloud.com if the device is lost or stolen.

Hot Tip

Apple-to-Apple messages are sent over the web and are not charged to your text message allowance. These iMessages appear in blue within the text thread.

Enable Messages and FaceTime

These apps enable free text, picture, voice and video communications with other iPhone/iPad/Mac users. Messages and FaceTime are two of the most used features on iPhones.

Touch ID

If you own an iPhone 5S, iPhone 6 or iPhone 6 Plus, you'll be asked to set up the Touch ID fingerprint sensor. This adds an extra layer of security to your

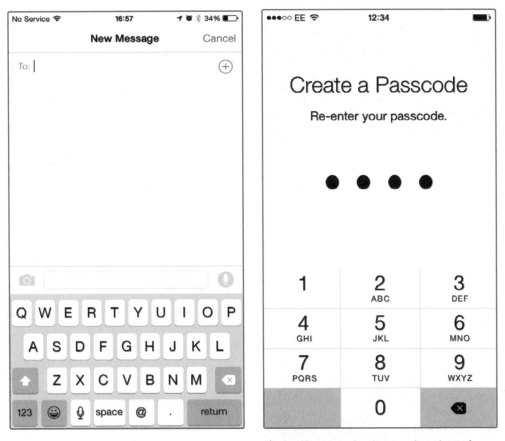

Above: The New Message screen on an iPhone 6.

Above: Adding a passcode prevents unauthorized parties from accessing your phone.

phone by requiring you to enter your print to access it. When prompted, place your finger or thumb on the sensor. You'll need to do this multiple times to capture the entire print. Once enabled, Touch ID can be used to unlock the phone, confirm app purchases and more.

Passcode

You should also enter a four-digit passcode (mandatory if using Touch ID), which is needed to access your phone when locked. Don't make the passcode something too obvious, such as your birth year.

Above: If Siri is enabled you'll be able to find information quickly just by using your voice.

Final Set-up Steps

You're almost there. Just a few more steps to go.

1. Activate your iCloud keychain. This saves all of your passwords and personal data across devices. Not a necessary step for new users.

2. Enable Siri, Apple's voice-powered personal assistant.

3. Choose whether you want to send App Analytics data to developers. (In our opinion, this is totally unnecessary.)

4. Choose between the standard and zoomed view. The zoomed view offers bigger icons and larger text (iPhone 6/6 Plus only).

5. That's it! Tap 'Get Started' to begin.

Hot Tip

Siri is a brilliant tool for finding information quickly. Just hold down the home button, wait for the tone and speak to get acquainted.

THE iOS HOMESCREEN

Once set-up is complete, you'll be taken straight to the iOS homescreen. This is your starting point for everything. In just a few taps, you'll be able to access all of the information on your phone from here.

APP ICONS

The iPhone comes with several pre-installed apps. Simply tapping one of the square icons will take you directly to an app. For example, to access the internet, tap the compass-like Safari icon; to enter the Music app, tap the note icon.

Hot Tip

In order to return to the homescreen and exit any app at any time, simply press the home button on the face of the iPhone.

Multiple Homescreens

If you swipe to the right with a finger, you'll see another homescreen with more apps. As you add more apps to your phone, these screens will fill up and be added to.

Above: Tap the icons on the homescreen to open apps.

Hot Tip

Drag one app on to another to create a new folder and give it a name. Perhaps all your games could go in one folder?

Above: App folders allow you to group apps for a tidier homescreen.

App Folders

Similar or related apps like Notes and Reminders can be placed in folders under names like Utilities. This makes the phone easier to navigate.

The Dock

The apps you use most often can be placed in the dock at the bottom of the screen, so they'll stay visible, whichever homescreen you're browsing.

The Status Bar

The top of the homescreen features several pieces of crucial information about your iPhone. Here are the main ones you'll see.

1. **Signal meter:** Shows the current strength of mobile signal.

2. **Wi-Fi/mobile data signal:** Shows whether and how you're connected to the internet.

3. **Time:** The current time of day.

4. **Location:** If location services are enabled, you'll see a compass arrow.

⑤ **Bluetooth**: If Bluetooth (*see page 76*) is switched on, an icon will appear here.

⑥ **Battery icon and percentage**: Gives you an idea about battery life.

Moving Apps

Moving apps around the homescreen and in and out of the dock is easy. Simply hold down one icon until they all begin to wobble, then drag individual apps around. Press the home button when finished.

Above: The status bar features crucial information.

Above: Hold down an app icon to make them all wobble.

KEY iOS HOMESCREEN TOOLS

We've covered the elements you can see on the homescreen, but there are a few others, such as the Control Center, Notifications and Spotlight Search, which are easily accessible from the iOS homescreen.

CONTROL CENTER

The iOS Settings app is home to the nuts and bolts of the operating system, but you can quickly adjust some settings from the Control Center. Swipe directly up from the bottom of the screen to bring up the menu. Here are the settings to which you can quickly toggle.

Hot Tip
Swipe up smoothly from just below the screen to access the Control Center.

1. **Airplane mode:** Switches off all cellular and internet activity. Perfect when flying.

2. **Wi-Fi:** Turn Wi-Fi on and off.

3. **Bluetooth:** Turn this connectivity tool on and off.

Right: The Control Center offers quick access to many key settings.

④ **Do not disturb**: Represented by the moon icon. DND settings can be adjusted in the main settings app.

⑤ **Portrait orientation lock**: Hitting this icon prevents the phone switching to landscape when turned on its side.

⑥ **Screen brightness**: Slide the meter left or right to alter this setting.

⑦ **Music**: These controls are handy when playing tunes, allowing you to play, stop, skip or change volume.

⑧ **AirDrop**: A tool for quickly sharing files with other Apple users.

⑨ **Torch, timer, calculator and camera**: Tapping these icons takes you straight to the corresponding app.

THE NOTIFICATIONS CENTER

Dragging down from just above the screen offers access to a 'Today' section featuring calendar appointments, alarm-clock settings, weather and upcoming birthdays. Tapping 'Notifications' shows all alerts from apps enabled in the Notifications settings. *See* page 49 for more on notifications.

Hot Tip

The Control Center and Notifications Center can even be accessed while the iPhone display is locked.

Below: The Notifications Center shows calendar appointments and weather.

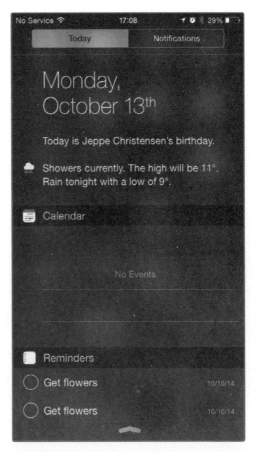

Above: Spotlight Search makes it easy to find content on your phone.

Spotlight Search

Dragging your finger in a downward motion on the touchscreen reveals a search field. Type here to quickly find a contact, an app, an email, a calendar event, an App Store listing or a Wikipedia page. Basically, it's a one-stop shop for searching the entire contents of your iPhone and beyond.

USEFUL iOS GESTURES

The iOS operating system is quite simple to navigate using the touchscreen, but in order for you to get the most out of the software you'll need to do more than just prod the display.

○ **Scroll:** You can move through menus, web pages and emails by scrolling a single finger up or down the page.

○ **Swipe:** A swipe left or right allows you to flick between homescreens, through photos, open menus in apps and so on.

○ **Pull down:** Dragging the screen down in apps like Mail refreshes the content of the page.

○ **Double-tap:** Zooms in/out on the content of a webpage or a photo.

○ **Two-finger spread:** Allows precise zoom-in controls.

○ **Two-finger pinch:** Allows more precise zoom-out controls.

○ **Pan:** Moving a single finger left/right /up/down allows you to look around environments like video games.

Left: You can refresh apps by dragging a finger down the screen.

SLEEP/WAKE/UNLOCK

After a certain amount of time inactive (usually a couple of minutes), or whenever you press the power button once, the display will go to sleep. This is to prevent others accessing the phone without your permission and to save battery life. If you have a passcode or Touch ID enabled, you'll have to unlock it before accessing the phone.

> ## Hot Tip
>
> **Swipe up from the camera icon on the lock screen to access the capture screen quickly without having to unlock the whole phone.**

- ○ **Sleep**: To put a display to sleep, tap the power button once.

- ○ **Wake**: To wake the display, hit the power button or the home button once.

Unlocking the iPhone

1. Wake the screen up.

2. If you have Touch ID enabled (iPhone 5S/6/6 Plus only), place the chosen finger or thumb on the home button sensor.

3. If the print is recognized, the phone will unlock.

4. Those without Touch ID will need to 'slide to unlock' and insert their four-digit passcode.

5. Those with Touch ID enabled can still use the passcode if more convenient.

Below: Swiping the camera icon opens the interface without unlocking the phone.

Swipe up

> slide to unlock

THE iOS KEYBOARD

The virtual keyboard within iOS is extremely simple to use, but essential for tapping out messages, emails, Facebook posts and everything in between. Here is a quick guide.

USING THE KEYBOARD

You entered your language preferences and typed in a few details while setting up the phone, so you know the keyboard appears automatically when you need to fill in information. Tapping within a field will load a cursor and summon the keyboard.

Learning Your Way Around the iOS Keyboard

The keyboard is laid out almost exactly like a computer keyboard. You'll see the QWERTY rows of letters, the space bar, return bar, backspace and shift.

- **Tapping shift once**: This will capitalize the first word of a letter.

- **Double-tapping shift:** This will enable Caps Lock.

Right: Tapping within a text field will automatically load the keyboard.

○ **Tapping the smiley face**: This will allow you to select emoji icons.

○ **Selecting '123'**: This loads numbers and symbols, while tapping the '#+=' key will show a second set of symbols.

○ **Tapping the microphone**: This will allow you to dictate text to the phone.

Below: In iOS 8 the keyboard guesses your next word.

iOS QuickType

In iOS 8, Apple has added a smart predictive text tool called SmartType, which guesses your next word based on how the sentence is developing and the person you're contacting. It'll also suggest words in response to questions. So, if you're asked whether you want to go to a movie or dinner, those words will be suggested and can be added with a single tap.

Alternative Keyboards

In iOS 8, Apple allows you to download a range of keyboards. For example, if you're used to using Swype or SwiftKey on Android, they can now be installed on your iPhone too. Find them in the App Store.

Copy and Paste Text

You can move text around different apps by selecting it, then copying and pasting it into a new app. Here's how.

1. Hold your finger down on a section of text. If it's a standalone message, you can just hit 'Copy'.

2. To select a section of text, such as a paragraph from a website in Safari, you'll need to drag the start and end markers to cover the section.

3. Browse to the new app, such as Messages or Mail, hold down a finger in the compose field and select 'Paste'.

Below: Copying and pasting text is an easy way to move text between apps.

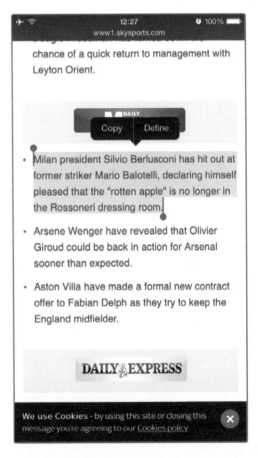

USING YOUR iPHONE

THE ANATOMY OF AN iPHONE

Before we get into making calls, sending texts, reading emails and the like, let's take a quick tour of your new iPhone's hardware.

HOME BUTTON

○ **Tap it once**: This will return you to the homescreen or wake the display if the phone is locked.

○ **Hold it down**: Holding it down will bring up Siri, the voice-controlled personal assistant.

○ **Double-tap it**: This will bring up the multitasking view and enable you to switch between apps easily.

○ **Touch ID fingerprint sensor**: If you have an iPhone 5S/6/6 Plus, the home button doubles up as a Touch ID fingerprint sensor.

Home button

SLEEP/WAKE AND POWER BUTTON

○ **Hold it down**: Hold it down to turn the device on and to bring up an on-screen slider to turn it off.

○ **Press it once**: Pressing it once wakes up the display or puts it to sleep.

1 **Ring/Silent switch:** To silence notifications, flick this switch.

2 **Volume buttons:** Alter in-call volume, notifications and media volume.

3 **iSight camera:** The iPhone's main camera can capture up to 8-megapixel stills and 1080p HD video.

4 **Receiver/Front microphone**

5 **3.5-mm headphone jack**

6 **Lightning charging port**

7 **Bottom speaker/Microphone**

8 **Antenna**

9 **Microphone**

10 **TrueTone flash:** Illuminates your photography subjects while doubling up as a flashlight.

Hot Tip

The volume buttons can also be used to activate the camera shutter when taking photos.

CONTACTS

To stay in touch with your nearest and dearest, you'll need their contact details on your iPhone.

No Service	17:27	23%
Groups	**Contacts**	+

Q Search

G

Tom **Grindley**

Dan **Gulliver**

Daniel **Gulliver**

jamie

Jamie **Gunn**

Tommy **Gunn**

Tommy **Gunn**

Dan **Gwilliam**

Dan **Gwilliam**

H

Haje

haje

Below: Access your friends, family and colleagues quickly through Contacts.

TRANSFERRING SIM CONTACTS

If you're buying your iPhone through a network provider, make sure they transfer all of your SIM information on to your new SIM card to ensure it's loaded with contacts from your previous device.

Transferring from a Google Account

If you're new to iOS, but have previously owned an Android smartphone, there's a good chance your contacts data is backed up in your Google Account. Synchronizing contacts from Google is easy to do.

1. Enter Settings > Mail, Contacts, Calendars.

2. Select Add Account and Choose Google.

3. Enter your Google account username and password.

4.   Ensure Contacts is toggled to on
     and save.

5.   Contacts from Google will
     immediately begin syncing.

Manually Adding a New Contact

You'll always be adding new contacts to
your iPhone and it's very easy to do so.

1.   Open the Contacts app on your iPhone.

2.   Hit the + button in the top-right corner.

3.   Fill in the name fields.

4.   Add in phone number, email,
     address, birthday, etc.

5.   Hit 'Done' to save the contact.

Adding Contacts from Other Areas

If you receive a phone call, an email or
a text from a new contact, you can easily
add that person to Contacts.

1.   In the Phone app, move to Recents.

2.   Select the 'i' icon next to the number.

Hot Tip

Hit the 'add photo' circle in the
New Contact page, snap a quick
pic and attach a photo.

No Service 🔊	18:35	🔋 23%
Cancel	**New Contact**	Done

add photo

First

Last

Company

⊕ add phone

⊕ add email

Ringtone	**Default**	›
Vibration	**Default**	›
Text Tone	**Default**	›
Vibration	**Default**	›

Above: You can add a new contact on your iPhone manually.

3. Select Create New Contact or Add to Existing Contact.

4. If it's the former, repeat the steps in the previous section.

5. If it's the latter, select the existing one from your contacts.

6. Select 'Done' to save the contact.

BACKING UP CONTACTS WITH iCLOUD

One way to safeguard your contacts is to use iCloud. Whenever you add a new contact it'll be automatically synced to your account. So, if you lose your phone or replace it with another iPhone, you won't lose your contacts. To ensure iCloud is backing up your contacts, head to Settings > iCloud and make sure the Contacts switch is toggled to the on position.

No Service 🗢	17:34	✈ 🌀 ✳ 21% 🔲

⟨ Settings　　**iCloud**

Chris Smith　　　　⟩

☁ Set Up Family Sharing…

Storage　　5.0 GB Available ⟩

☁ iCloud Drive　　Off ⟩

✿ Photos　　On ⟩

✉ Mail

👤 Contacts

▦ Calendars

☰ Reminders

🧭 Safari

Above: iCloud can back up your contacts and other important data.

Hot Tip

Head to iCloud.com and log in using your Apple ID to view all of your contacts on the web.

MAKING AND RECEIVING CALLS

With your contacts safely stowed on the iPhone, you can begin interacting with them. We'll deal with phone calls in this section.

MAKING CALLS WITH THE PHONE APP

The pre-installed Phone app is the hub for making calls, although you can also make some from other areas of the phone (such as the Contacts, Messages and Email apps). Entering the Phone app presents the following options:

- **Favourites**: Shortcuts to favourite contacts. Hit the '+' icon to add them.

- **Recents**: Lists calls made, received and missed in chronological order; tap a number to call it.

- **Contacts**: Gives access to your contacts book; tap a contact and select a number to call it.

- **Keypad**: Here, you can enter a number manually and hit the green button to call it.

- **Voicemail**: Tap the tape reel to call your voicemail.

Above: You can simply dial numbers on the iPhone's keypad.

MAKING CALLS FROM OTHER APPS

In any app where you see a phone number or a contact, you can tap it to directly call that number.

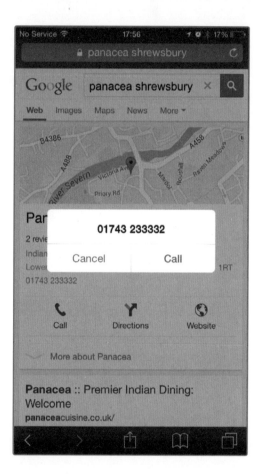

- **Mail**: Tap a phone number in an email signature and select 'Call' from the pop-up notification. More often than not, they'll be underlined in blue.

- **Messages**: Within a message thread, hit 'Details' and tap the phone icon to call.

- **Safari**: If searching for a restaurant, for example, you can tap the phone number listed in order to call directly.

Right: You can make calls from other apps like Safari by tapping numbers and links.

Hot Tip

Emergency calls can be made from the lock screen. Wake the display and hit 'Emergency' in the bottom-left corner to access the keypad.

ANSWERING AND DECLINING CALLS

'Ring! Ring! Ring! Ring!' (or whatever tone you've chosen). You've got an incoming call. What do you do to answer or reject the call? When the phone rings, you'll see a number of options.

○ **Accept**: The green icon allows you to answer the call. If the phone is unlocked, simply tap this. If it is locked, drag the slider to answer.

○ **Decline**: To send the call directly to voicemail, tap or slide the red button.

○ **Message**: (iOS 8 only) If you'd rather reply with a text than answer the call, tap Message to head to a compose screen. The call will go to voicemail.

○ **Remind**: Tapping this will also decline the call, but will ask you to set a reminder to call the person back. You'll receive a notification when that time comes.

○ **Silence the call**: You can allow the call to ring out by holding the minus volume button or flicking the silent switch.

Below: iOS gives you multiple options when a call comes in.

Hot Tip

Pressing the home button answers a call. Pressing and holding for a couple of seconds declines it.

The In-call Screen

So you hit that green button to place or answer a call. You can now simply speak to the person on the other end of the phone, but there are more options on the in-call screen:

- **Mute**: Mutes your voice if you only want to listen, not speak.

- **Keypad**: Accesses the keyboard for use with automated phone menus.

- **Speaker**: Places the call on speakerphone, allowing you to go hands free.

- **Red phone icon**: Hang up the call.

Voicemail

You can set up an answerphone message by hitting the Voicemail tab in the Phone app. The process will differ for each mobile network, so follow the audio instructions. When you receive a voicemail, you will receive a notification or alert, and a red badge will also appear next to the Voicemail tab.

Left: The iOS in-call options.

MESSAGING

Text messaging has come a long way since the first phones that made this form of communication so much a part of our everyday lives. The Messages app allows users so much flexibility. There are two main ways to send messages: via text messages and iMessages.

TEXT MESSAGES

If you're texting someone on a different platform to iOS (Android, Windows Phone, etc.), messages will be sent as a traditional text message.

iMESSAGE

iMessages can be exchanged freely between iOS users. They are sent over the internet via mobile internet (3G or 4G) or Wi-Fi, and are attached to your Apple ID and phone number. iMessages allow you to send text, photos, video clips and audio files.

The Messages App

Opening the Messages app opens a list of conversations. You can scroll up and down this list or type in the search box to find

Right: Find the person you want to message through Contacts.

●●○○○ EE 📶	11:19 AM	✈ 🔋 88% 🔋
Groups	**All Contacts**	+

🔍 Search

H

Steve **Hunter**

I

Ida

Serafino **Ingardia**

Lindsay **Inglesby**

Ingrid

Will **Ireland**

Ivan

J

J&T. GB Phone

Mike **Jackson**

A B C D E F G H I J K L M N O P Q R S T U V W X Y Z #

the relevant thread. Tapping a thread will open the conversation thread between you and the other person(s).

Composing/Sending a Message

It's easy to compose and send a text message or iMessage; here's how:

Below: iMessages appear in blue.

1. Hit the pen and paper icon in the top-right corner.

2. Begin typing the name/number of the contact in the To: field to load suggestions.

3. Select the correct suggested contact from the list or type in the full number.

4. Type the message in the Compose field.

Hot Tip

iMessages sent are depicted by a blue bubble, whereas regular text messages are shown in green. The Compose field shows how it'll be sent before you begin typing.

5. Press Send when you're ready. iMessages will show a Delivered notification.

6. If a message has not sent, you'll see a red exclamation mark. Tap this to 'Try Again' or 'Send as Text Message'.

Adding Photos/ Videos to iMessages

1. Tap the camera icon in the bottom-left corner of a conversation thread. This will present a number of options.

2. In iOS 8, you'll see a carousel of the most recent photos from your Photos app. Tap to attach. You can also choose 'Photo Library' to find it manually.

3. 'Take Photo or Video' will load the Camera app. Capture the photo or video, select 'Use Photo' or 'Retake' until you're happy with it.

Sending Tap to Talk Audio iMessages

You can record an audio message and send it through iMessage. Press and hold the microphone icon in the bottom-right corner to begin recording. When

Below: Adding photos or video to iMessages is easy.

you've finished speaking, release the mic button and select the up arrow to send the audio. In iOS 8, you can listen to an audio message just by lifting the phone to your ear!

Reading Messages

If you send a message, hopefully you'll get one in return. When the reply arrives, it will be delivered to your phone in the form of a notification. If your phone is locked, the notification will appear on the lock screen.

1. You can head straight to the message by swiping the notification to the right.

2. If the phone is unlocked, you'll get an alert-style notification, where you can select 'Reply', or 'Cancel' to dismiss for now.

3. You can also open the Messages app and browse straight to the thread.

Hot Tip

In iOS 8, tapping 'Reply' from an alert-style notification allows you to tap out a quick reply right there and then without having to enter the Messages app.

Above: You can reply directly from message alerts in iOS 8.

FACETIME

Why restrict yourself to voice calls or texts when you can see your friends and family live and in living colour? Through the FaceTime app, you can make free (over the internet) video or audio calls to anyone else also using an iOS device.

USING FACETIME

FaceTime is the green and white video camera icon on the iPhone homescreen. Tap this to enter the app. The first time you use it, you may have to sign in using your Apple ID.

Hot Tip

Can't find your keys at night? Swipe up to load the Control Center and hit the Flashlight icon for a little illumination.

FaceTime Video Calls

Starting a FaceTime call is very straightforward:

1. Open the FaceTime app.

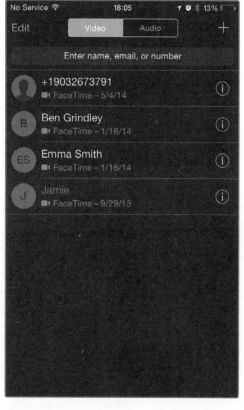

Above: You can call other iPhone users using FaceTime video or audio.

2. Enter a name, email address or phone number in the field, or hit the + icon to choose from your contacts.

3. Select the video icon to begin the call.

4. Your image will appear in the bottom corner (thanks to the front-facing camera), while the recipient will appear in a larger window on the screen.

FaceTime Audio

Making FaceTime calls over Wi-Fi means you won't pay call charges on your mobile phone bill. Select the phone icon rather than the video camera to make an audio call.

Hot Tip

You can call someone on FaceTime direct from a contact page in the Contacts app or within Messages.

Right: FaceTime video chats are a fun way to communicate with friends and family.

NOTIFICATIONS

The iPhone has many ways of alerting you of calls missed, messages and emails received, as well as notifying you of Facebook activity and so on.

SELECTING NOTIFICATION STYLES

A lot of apps have default notification styles. However, you can customize them for each individual app using Settings > Notifications. Here, you can choose whether they appear on the lock screen and, among other things, the alert style when the phone's unlocked.

Lock-screen Notifications

You're notified of messages even if your screen is locked. Missed calls, emails and

Hot Tip

You can swipe right on a lock-screen notification to be taken directly to the app.

No Service 📶	18:11	🔋 11%

< Notifications   Facebook

Allow Notifications   ⬤

Show in Notification Center   5 >

Sounds   ⬤

Badge App Icon   ⬤

Show on Lock Screen   ⬤

Show alerts on the lock screen, and in Notification Center when it is accessed from the lock screen.

ALERT STYLE WHEN UNLOCKED

None   Banners   Alerts

Alerts require an action before proceeding.
Banners appear at the top of the screen and go away

Above: You can set your notification preferences in Settings.

so on are set to 'Show On Lock Screen' by default. You can toggle this by browsing to Settings > Notifications > App (for example, Mail).

Banner Notifications

Some apps send you banners to alert you to incoming information. These appear at the top of the screen when the phone is unlocked and quickly disappear. You can tap them to interact with the alert or ignore.

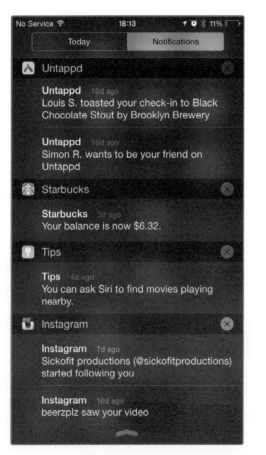

Alert-style Notifications

Alert-style notifications come through when the phone is unlocked, and are useful for apps where it's important you see the notification as soon as it comes through. The alert stays on the screen until you interact with it.

Notifications Center

We mentioned this in the first chapter (see page 25). Swiping down from the top of the screen reveals the most recent notifications from your favourite apps.

Badges on App Icons

Another way iOS lets you know that you've received a notification is a red badge in the top-right corner of an app icon on the homescreen. For example, if you have three unread emails, you'll see a '3' badge attached to the app.

Left: Alerts from your favourite apps sit in the Notifications Center.

Sounds

An incoming call will be notified by a default ringtone. If you wish to change this to something more aurally pleasing, head to Settings > Notifications > Phone > Notification Sound and choose from the list.

Hot Tip

You can also buy custom ringtones. Hit the Store link from within the ringtone selection screen.

Below: A red badge next to an icon shows the number of unread notifications.

CUSTOMIZING YOUR PHONE

Your iPhone may look the same as others' on the outside, but on the inside, the world is your oyster. You can customize the look and feel of the software, depending on how you use your phone.

WALLPAPER

There's no reason to stick to the default iOS decoration. You can choose from a selection of attractive designs as well as your own photos.

Above: Changing the wallpaper can brighten up your iPhone experience.

Changing the Wallpaper

Head to the Settings app and select 'Wallpaper' ('Wallpaper & Brightness' in iOS 7). This will display the items currently occupying the homescreen.

1. Tap 'Choose a New Wallpaper'.

2. You can select 'Dynamic' wallpapers (which appear to move as you tilt the screen) or 'Stills'.

3. Below, you'll see your photo albums, tap to browse and select.

4. Pick the new wallpaper and choose 'Set'.

5. Choose 'Set Wallpaper/Lock Screen/Both' (a slightly different command to what appears in iOS 7).

CUSTOMIZING HOMESCREENS

Naturally, you want the apps you use most to be the easiest to reach. That means placing them in the dock and on the first iOS homescreen. That way, you won't be swiping through multiple screens to find them.

Rearranging Apps on the Homescreen

1. Hold down an app and all of the apps will begin jiggling while displaying little crosses above them.

2. Simply drag an app icon to where you'd like it to stay.

3. If it's one of your four most-used apps, drag it into the dock.

4. Press the home button when complete.

Above: You can drag and drop apps to different areas of the homescreen.

BRIGHTNESS

If you're using your phone in bright sunlight, you'll want to increase the visibility. At night, brightness will come way down. Brightness can be altered from the Control Center by swiping up from the homescreen.

Above: It's quick and easy to adjust screen brightness in the Control Center.

Auto-brightness

If enabled, the Auto-brightness setting adjusts the display based on the lighting conditions. Head to Settings > Display & Brightness to turn on Auto-brightness.

Text Size and Bold Text

If the text is a little small on your iPhone, head to Settings > Display & Brightness > Text Size and drag the slider to increase or decrease the size. You can also make the text bolder here, by toggling the switch.

Zoomed View
(iPhone 6/6 Plus only)

Make app icons and text larger or smaller by switching between the Standard and Zoom View. Head to Settings > Display & Brightness > Display Zoom.

Above: Using the zoomed view on iPhone 6/Plus allows users to make app icons larger.

Hot Tip

In iOS 8, these features are found in Settings > Display & Brightness. In iOS 7, this is called the Wallpaper & Brightness menu.

USING THE INTERNET

CONNECTING TO THE INTERNET

Before we can start browsing the internet, sending emails, downloading apps and streaming music and video, we must establish a connection to the internet.

WI-FI AND MOBILE DATA

In the first chapter, we connected to the internet in order to register the iPhone and complete the set-up (*see page 16*). To do this, we connected to a Wi-Fi network or used mobile data. These are the two main ways to connect to the internet using an iPhone.

Hot Tip

Mobile data allowances are usually limited, so connect to a Wi-Fi network wherever possible.

Connecting to a Wi-Fi Network

Enter the Settings app and select Wi-Fi. Ensure the switch is toggled to on (you can

Left: Connecting to the internet allows you to browse the web through Safari.

also turn it on/off with a single tap in the Control Center). If you're at home, the Wi-Fi network name and password will be on a label on the modem.

1. Pick the Wi-Fi network from the list.

2. If a password is required, enter it when prompted and select 'Join'.

3. If the password is accepted, you'll see the Wi-Fi meter appear in the status bar.

4. Open Safari and type a web address (for example, bbc.co.uk) to test the connection.

Connecting to Public Wi-Fi

Most cafés, restaurants, bars and public spaces now offer free Wi-Fi to visitors. You'll be able to find the network (usually named after the establishment) within the 'Connect to Network' list. Some networks require you to log in or accept terms and conditions, while others will be password-protected. Ask a member of staff for the password.

Mobile Data

Mobile data allows you to have constant connectivity to the internet when out and

Hot Tip

iOS will remember where you have logged on to Wi-Fi networks and automatically connect next time you are within range.

Below: To connect to a Wi-Fi network, you'll need the network name and password.

No Service 🔋	21:31	✈ ⚙ ☀ 100% 🔋
‹ Settings	**Wi-Fi**	

| Wi-Fi | ⬤◯ |
| ✓ BTHub3-NTP3 | 🔒 🔋 ⓘ |

PERSONAL HOTSPOTS

| Chris's iPhone | •••• 3G 🔋 🔗 |

CHOOSE A NETWORK... 🔅

BTWifi-with-FON	🔋 ⓘ
BTWifi-X	🔒 🔋 ⓘ
Other...	

| Ask to Join Networks | ◯ |

Known networks will be joined automatically. If no known networks are available, you will have to manually select a network.

about and out of Wi-Fi range. Usually some mobile data comes bundled into your mobile contract or pay-as-you-go deal. The more you pay, the more data you'll get. Talk to your network provider about your allowance and usage habits.

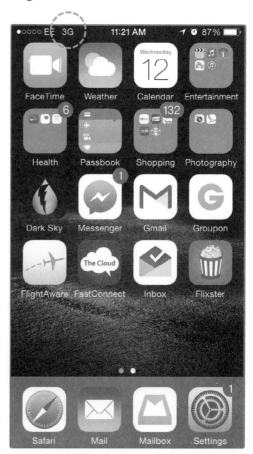

Above: The speed of your mobile data connection appears in the status bar; in this instance, the phone is connected to the 3G network.

Data Speeds

Depending on where you are in the country and the strength of the connection, you'll receive different levels of mobile data speeds. The current speed will be represented in the data bar.

○ **E**: The 2G Edge network is very slow, suitable for basic web browsing and emailing.

○ **3G**: Gives much faster connectivity. Can be used to stream music and download apps.

○ **4G**: The fastest available speeds, often called LTE. 4G data deals are often a little more expensive.

Below: You can configure mobile data connectivity within the Settings app.

No Service 📶	22:09	✈ ⌾ ⁂ 96% 🔋
‹ Settings	**Cellular**	

Cellular Data ⬤

Enable LTE   Voice & Data ›

Turn off cellular data to restrict all data to Wi-Fi, including email, web browsing, and push notifications.

Roaming   Off ›

Personal Hotspot   Off ›

CALL TIME

Current Period   6 Hours, 38 Minutes

Lifetime   6 Hours, 38 Minutes

CELLULAR DATA USAGE

Current Period   31.5 GB

Current Period Roaming   0 bytes

Hot Tip

If your battery life is flagging, switch off 4G connectivity and use 3G to conserve life. Head to Settings > Cellular > Enable 4G and toggle to the off position.

BROWSING THE WORLD WIDE WEB

Now we're connected to the internet, we can start consuming all of that great content. You can make Google searches, catch up on the news, find recipes, check the football scores and much more.

THE SAFARI APP

The default iOS app for browsing the internet is Safari. It allows you to load web pages, store your favourites, share interesting pages and more besides.

Hot Tip

Tapping a web link from within another app, like Messages, Mail or Calendar, will automatically open the page in Safari.

Loading a Web Page or Performing a Web Search

Open the Safari application and tap the 'Search web or enter site name' field to summon the iOS keyboard. You can then

Left: Safari allows you to browse the web once connected to the internet.

type a search term (e.g. Restaurants in Liverpool) or a web URL (e.g. Apple.com) and select 'Go'.

Interacting with Webpages

Once a page has loaded, there are several ways to interact with it:

- **Back/Forward arrows**: Move to the previous/next page.

- **Tap link**: Tap other web links onscreen to navigate to that page.

- **Scroll**: Slowly swipe a finger up and down to move through the content.

- **Double-tap**: Zoom in on a specific area.

- **Spread/Pinch with two fingers**: Zoom in and out.

- **Press and hold a link**: Add to bookmarks, open in new tab.

Right: You can zoom in on pages by spreading two fingers on the touchscreen.

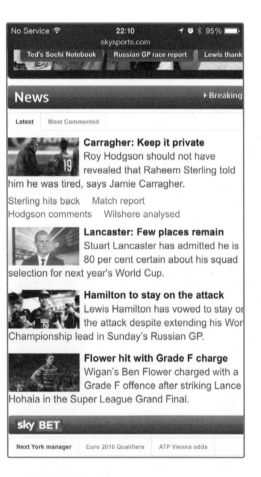

Hot Tip

The pages you visit most often will appear as icons on the Safari start page.

Share Links, Add Bookmarks, Save to Reading List

Tapping the share icon at the foot of the Safari window (the page with the arrow pointing up) presents lots of options for webpages.

- **Share**: If you find an article you want to forward on, you can send to contacts via Message or Mail. Selecting these will load a blank message or email containing the link. If you want to share with your social media circles, select Twitter or Facebook. We'll deal with setting these up later.

Above: Tapping the share icon opens up a wealth of options.

- **Add Bookmark**: Saves the link if you're going to want to access it again.

- **Add to Reading List**: If you don't have time to read the page right now, tap this to add it to your reading list.

- **Add to Homescreen**: If it's a page you look at often, you can add a direct link to the homescreen, via an icon.

- **Copy**: Copy the link for pasting in another app not listed.

Accessing Saved Links

Items you've bookmarked or saved to the reading list can be accessed at any time, by tapping the book icon at the foot of the Safari page.

Opening New Safari Windows

You don't have to limit your activity to the one browser window. You can tap the windows icon (overlapping pages) in the bottom-right corner and open a new page.

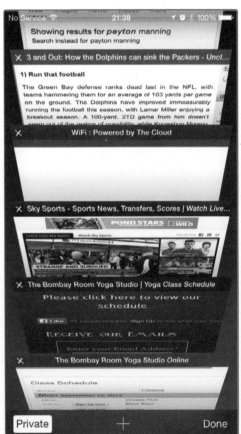

Above: You can have multiple Safari windows open at one time.

Hot Tip

You can search Google from the Spotlight app on your iPhone. Drag down on the homescreen and begin typing. Hit Search web when complete.

EMAIL

You can compose, send, receive and reply to emails directly from your iPhone. All you need is to be connected to the internet, and you set up your email accounts using the Apple Mail app, which is represented by an envelope icon in the iOS dock.

CONFIGURING EMAIL USING THE MAIL APP

When you first open the Mail app, you'll be asked to choose an account from one of the popular providers, like Google's Gmail, Yahoo! Mail or Microsoft Outlook.

1. Select your provider from the list. In this case, we'll use Gmail.

2. Insert your name (this will be what recipients see when they receive your email), Gmail email address and the password associated with the account.

3. Add a description, for example, My Gmail account.

Left: The iPhone Mail app supports all of the leading providers.

Sharing Data with Other Apps

The Apple Mail app is great, as it can play nice with many other iOS apps. On the final screen before setting up the app, you'll be asked whether you want to share information from your email account with other iOS apps.

- **Contacts**: Switching Contacts to the on position will sync your email contacts to your iPhone contacts book.

- **Calendars**: Enabling your calendars will mean all appointments made through your email account will be synced back to the iOS Calendar app.

> ### Hot Tip
>
> **To add more accounts, head to Settings > Mail, Contacts, Calendars > Add Account.**

Sending an Email

Tapping the 'pen and paper' icon within the Mail app summons a new window, from which a new email can be sent. Here's how.

Right: Turning on Contacts when setting up Mail will sync them to your Contacts app.

No Service 🗢	21:43	🢁 🅾 ⁜ 100% ▬
‹ Mail…	**Gmail**	

GMAIL

Account	cjsfreelance@gmail.com ›

✉	Mail	
☻	Contacts	
▦	Calendars	
▤	Notes	

Delete Account

1. Begin typing the recipient's name or email address in the To: field. Suggestions will load from contacts. Alternatively, tap the + symbol to add from Contacts.

2. Fill in the subject line with a brief description of the email's purpose.

3. Tap the compose field (the blank area under the subject line) to begin typing your email.

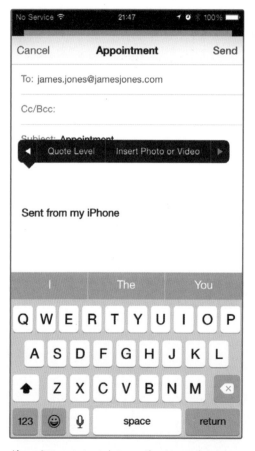

4. To add a media attachment, hold down your finger in the compose field, tap the right arrow and select 'Insert Photo or Video'.

5. When complete, press send and you'll be greeted with a 'whoosh' sound to signify it's on its way.

Hot Tip

You can check the email has been sent by navigating to the Sent folder within the Mail app.

Above: It is easy to insert photos or videos into email messages.

Your Mail Inbox

Emails will be listed in order, with the most recently received first. Each item on the list will show an email preview containing the sender, the subject line, the time/date the email was sent and a brief preview of the text.

Useful Mail Gestures

The Mail app gestures differ slightly in iOS 7 and iOS 8. From the inbox list, you can swipe a message to perform actions quickly. For example, in iOS 8, a long swipe right will send the email to the trash, while in iOS 7, this is performed via a swipe left. Other gestures include:

- **Swipe left**: Mark as unread.

- **Short flick right**: In iOS 8, this displays options to send to trash, flag for later viewing, or you can select More for other options. This feature isn't present in the iOS 7 Mail app.

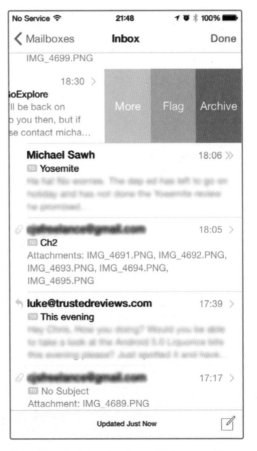

Above: You can swipe email previews quickly to access options.

Hot Tip

To delete multiple emails, hit 'Edit' within a mailbox, mark the emails and delete them.

No Service 📶   21:50   ↑ 🔘 ✳ 100% ▰▰▰▰

< Inbox   **Thread**   Edit

Heat   2 items

Teresa Coldwell   15:53 >
🔲 Re: Heat

Teresa Coldwell   Saturday >
🔲 Heat

Updated Just Now   ✎

Viewing Email

Tap an email in the inbox. If the email is the latest in a thread, you'll also see previous emails below. Unread emails will be identified by a blue dot. Tap to read the contents and interact with the email.

Replying to Email

Within an email message, tap the left-facing arrow to respond. You can choose 'Reply' (to reply to the sender), 'Reply All' to respond to others who may be copied in, or 'Forward' to send it on to a third party. Here, you can add your response in the compose field and hit 'Send' when you're done.

Sending Mail from Other Apps

One of the great things about the Mail app is the ability to transition into it from other apps. In the previous section, we talked about sharing Safari web links via the share button. Here are a couple of others.

- **Photos:** Select the photo(s) you wish to send. Hit the share button and select Mail. This will load a new email window with the photo(s) attached.

- **Contacts:** Tap a contact's email address to begin an email addressed to them.

Receiving Email

Every time an email comes through, you'll receive a notification based on the preferences set in Settings > Notifications > Mail. You'll also see a red badge icon on the mail app when unread mails are sitting in your inbox. You can choose how often the app goes looking for new mail.

Below: You can attach a photo to a new email message directly from the Photos app.

APPLE MAPS

iOS has a built-in Maps application that can provide you with driving, walking, cycling and public transport directions, while also replacing your standalone satnav unit with voice-powered turn-by-turn directions.

USING APPLE MAPS

When you open the Maps app for the first time, you'll be transported directly to your current location, highlighted by a red pin and a pop-up naming that location. If it's your house, you should see your address.

Search for a Location

Simply tap in the search field and begin typing an address to load suggestions. It could be a local restaurant or the nearest service station. Confirm which suggestion is the correct location. Alternatively, you can hit 'My Favourites' to look at recent locations, or search from your contacts. The Maps app will take you directly there.

Get Directions

Once you've identified where you're heading, simply tap the right-turn arrow

Left: Apple Maps makes it easy to find nearby restaurants and attractions.

in the top-left corner to get directions from your current location. You'll see the entire route onscreen, along with the distance and time it'll take to get there. At the top of the screen, you can switch between driving and walking directions.

Below: Apple Maps offers driving and walking directions to your destination.

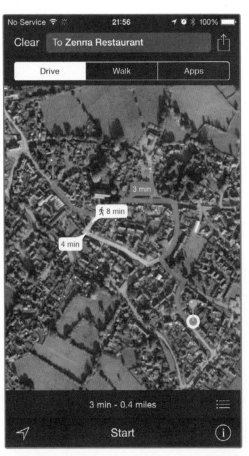

Hot Tip

If you search for nearby restaurants, some of the results will feature reviews powered by the Yelp app.

Hot Tip

Tap the compass arrow at any time to show your current location on the screen.

Turn-by-turn Directions

The Apple Maps app can act like a traditional satnav, offering voice-aided, turn-by-turn directions to your final destination. Once you've chosen your preferred route, press 'Start' to load the satnav interface and listen to the instructions. To view text-based instructions, tap the list icon in the bottom-right corner.

Hot Tip

To use Maps, the phone's GPS connection must be switched on. Go to Settings > Location Services and ensure they're switched on.

Using Maps with Other Apps

Like Mail, Maps is another app that integrates well with others.

- **Messages & Mail**: If someone sends a message or an email containing an address, tap the address to load it directly into the Maps app.

Left: Turn-by-turn navigation in Apple Maps can replace your satnav.

- **Safari**: On a Safari webpage, if an address is listed, you can tap that message to load it in Maps.

- **Calendar**: Heading to a meeting? Look at the appointment in your Calendar app, then tap the location to load the directions in Maps.

- **Siri**: You can ask Siri to 'Get directions to' your location and the turn-by-turn portion of the app will load instantly. Hold down the home button and speak.

Hot Tip

You can add any location to your Contacts book. Tap the red pin and hit Create New Contact or Add To Existing Contact.

No Service   22:00   98%

"Can you get me directions to Shrewsbury"
tap to edit

Getting directions to Shrewsbury...

Right: Hold down the home button and ask Siri for directions. Maps will load instantly.

OTHER WAYS TO CONNECT

There are plenty of other ways you can use your iPhone to wirelessly connect with other devices and the outside world. For example, the iPhone is equipped with Bluetooth and AirPlay technology.

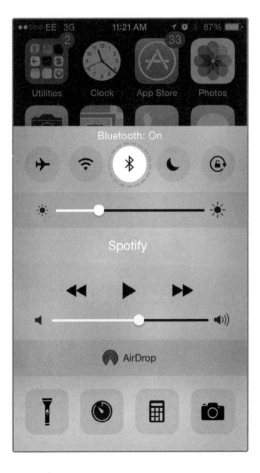

BLUETOOTH

Bluetooth is a low-powered technology that allows you to connect with other devices. For example, if you wear a fitness tracker or use a hands-free headset, or have Bluetooth-enabled speakers, you can send data or media directly to them from your iPhone.

Hot Tip

You can only connect one device via Bluetooth at a time.

Pairing via Bluetooth

Firstly, make sure your Bluetooth is switched on. This can be quickly toggled on/off in the Control Center. Now, you

Left: Bluetooth settings are accessible through the Control Center.

must follow the instructions that came with the accessory itself to make it 'discoverable' by other devices. Open Bluetooth in the iOS Settings and 'Pair the devices' (you may have to enter a passkey specified by the device).

APPLE AIRPLAY

AirPlay is Apple's Wi-Fi-based media-streaming platform, which allows you to send audio or video content to an Apple TV set-top box or AirPlay-enabled speakers.

Connecting via AirPlay

When you're on the same Wi-Fi network as an AirPlay-enabled device, the AirPlay option will appear in the Control Center. Tap AirPlay to choose the device and the video/audio will be sent.

APPS

WHAT IS AN APP?

An app is a self-contained mini program on your iPhone that allows you to perform certain functions. There are plenty of apps built into your iPhone, like Mail and Messages. However, through the App Store, you can download countless new ones to your iPhone.

WORKING WITH APPS

We've already done lots of work within apps throughout this book, opening them up by tapping the icons. Here are a few useful tips for managing applications.

iOS Multitasking

With iOS, it is easy to switch between your favourite apps. Double-tap the home button to bring up the multitasking view.

Closing Apps

The more apps that are open, the slower your phone works and the more battery life is consumed. There's an easy trick for quitting those apps you're not using: double-tap the home button to launch the multitasking view and swipe the app cards up off the top of the display.

Left: You might want to put entertainment-based apps in a single folder.

Hot Tip

Use up to three fingers and close multiple apps per swipe.

Below: Closing down apps you're not using can help conserve battery life.

Deleting Apps

iPhones range from 16 GB to 128 GB in size, meaning that you may have to delete some of your less-used apps to free up space from time to time.

1. Press and hold an app on the home screen until the icons begin to jiggle.

2. Tap the 'X' to delete the app.

3. Hit 'Delete' to confirm.

DOWNLOADING APPS

The iPhone comes loaded with loads of apps like Mail, Messages, Maps and Safari, but there are hundreds, even thousands more that you can download from the App Store.

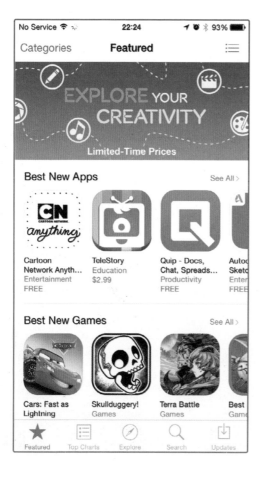

THE APP STORE

The Apple App Store is your one-stop shop for filling your phone with awesome social media apps, photo-sharing tools, great touchscreen games and music-streaming apps to name but a few. Tap the App Store icon on the homescreen to get started.

Hot Tip

Apps over 50 MB in size have to be downloaded over Wi-Fi. This can be annoying if you're out and about, but can save your data allowance.

Finding Apps

Loading the App Store will take you to the featured section, which offers a snapshot of the featured new apps.

Left: All apps are downloaded from the App Store.

○ **Categories**: Select 'Categories' to browse to specific areas.

○ **Top Charts**: The 'Top Charts' option lists the current most popular apps in the Store.

○ **Search**: If you know what you're looking for, hit the Search tab and type in the name, for example, Angry Birds.

Downloading Apps

Once you've found the app you want to download, take a look at the price description and user ratings. To download, just do the following:

Below: You need to enter your Apple ID passcode to confirm an app purchase.

1. Tap the Free/Price icon.

2. Confirm the purchase by entering your passcode (or Touch ID print).

3. Wait for the app to download (you can see the progress on the homescreen).

4. The app will appear on your homescreen and can be opened when the download is complete.

Updating Apps

Developers are constantly updating their apps with new features, bug fixes, new gaming levels and more. It's easy to make sure you have the newest version.

1. Open the App Store and head to the Updates tab (the number of apps that require an update will be indicated by a red badge).

2. Scan available updates and update apps individually.

In-app Purchases

Some apps are free to download, while others cost a couple of pounds or so. Other apps contain in-app purchases, which enable you to unlock new content, levels, characters and features. It'll also allow you to buy virtual coins to spend within video games.

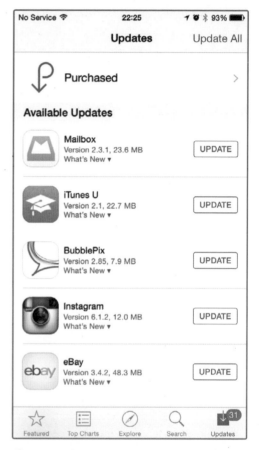

Above: App updates can bring new features and crush bugs.

Hot Tip

If an app is crashing a lot, check to see if there's an update available. That almost always fixes the problem.

Reinstalling Apps

If you have to delete an app you've paid for or want to install it on a new device, don't worry, you don't have to pay again. All app purchases are remembered and can be re-downloaded.

1. Open the App Store > Updates.

2. Browse to Purchased > Not on This iPhone.

3. Download the apps you wish to reinstall.

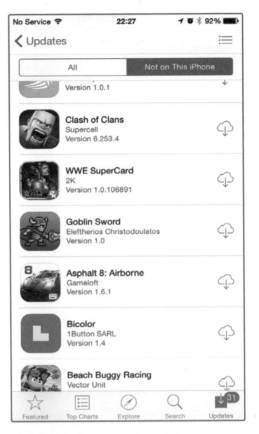

Above: The Purchased section of the App Store features apps you've previously downloaded.

BUILT-IN APPS

The iPhone comes loaded with a couple of dozen apps that'll get you through the basics. We've discussed some of these in great detail already, but here are some of the other tools to help you through the day.

No Service	22:29	92%
Cancel	**New Event**	Add

Title

Location

All-day

Starts   Oct 13, 2014   22:00

Ends   23:00

Repeat   Never >

Travel Time   None >

Q W E R T Y U I O P
A S D F G H J K L
Z X C V B N M
123   space   return

Above: You can arrange meetings and invite people via the Calendar app.

Hot Tip

You can set a location-based reminder. So, for example, if you're calling at the supermarket on the way home, you can set a reminder to buy butter when you get there.

Calendar

Make appointments through your phone and receive a notification to remind you before the event. Appointments from your email account are also incorporated. You can even link it to your Facebook account so you remember everyone's birthdays.

To add an appointment manually, open the Calendar app, tap the '+' button and fill in details like time, location and alert style. You can also invite people by typing in email addresses.

Reminders

Your own personal to-do list!

1. Open the app and hit the '+' button to start a new list.

2. Name the list and give it a colour code.

3. Type items you need to complete and press enter.

4. As you tick them off, tap the circle next to the item.

5. Tap the 'i' icon to set a reminder (via a notification on your phone).

Notes

This is a simple note-taking app, which allows you to jot down thoughts. Simply tap 'New' and begin typing. iOS will automatically save your note and sync it to other devices via iCloud.

Voice Memos

If you'd rather record your thoughts, or even a lecture or an interview, you can use the Voice Memos app. Simply hit the record button to start.

Clock

iPhones tend to replace the need for multiple gadgets. Digital cameras and satnavs are certainly less necessary, these days, as are alarm clocks. You can use the Clock app for this, which also features a stopwatch, timer and world clock.

Weather

Here, you can see the weather in your current location as well as adding places around the world.

Right: The weather app tells you whether you're likely to need an umbrella.

Hot Tip

Treat yourself to a really swish weather app and download Dark Sky. It's a paid-for app, but the notifications when it's about to rain can be day savers!

SIRI

Siri is the voice-powered personal assistant which can be used for setting reminders, finding directions, searching the web, setting appointments, opening maps, sending messages, posting to Facebook and much more. You must be connected to the internet in order to use Siri.

USING SIRI

The idea behind Siri is to fire questions/commands at her by holding down the home button. Replies will come via a spoken response, or she will open an app or provide a web link.

Hot Tip

iOS 8 brings a new 'Hey Siri' setting, which allows you to use it without holding down the home button. You must be connected to a power source though.

Using Siri to Answer Questions

Siri is an all-knowing, interactive tool. For example, if you're looking to answer

Left: You can ask Siri to post to Facebook on your behalf.

a specific question like 'Where was Charles Darwin born?', she can deliver that information without leaving the interface, or provide a link to a Wikipedia page.

Other Uses for Siri

Hold down the home button and give these a try.

○ **'Post to Facebook'**: You can dictate a status update to Siri, check it and post.

○ **'Take me home Siri'**: Loads turn-by-turn directions to your home address in the Maps app.

○ **'Call Mum'**: This will instantly begin a call.

○ **'Tell Chris I'm running late'**: Sends a message to a contact.

○ **'Remind me to...'**: Ask Siri to add something to Reminders. You can even set location-based reminders, like 'Remind me to call Mum when I get home.'

○ **'What's the weather going to be like tomorrow?'**: Loads relevant weather information.

Right: You can ask Siri for a weather forecast.

- **'Play The Killers'**: Begins playing music from your library.

- **'Did Liverpool win last night?'**: Siri even knows the football scores.

For more information on how you can use Siri, tap the question mark in the bottom-left corner of the interface.

Hot Tip

Siri has a sense of humour too. Ask her the meaning of life and she'll tell you that 'All evidence points to chocolate.' Have some fun with it!

No Service 22:40 89%

"When do Liverpool play next"
tap to edit

The Liverpool - Queens Park Rangers game is Sunday at 13:30:

English Premier League Schedule

Sun, Oct 19, 2014   TV: NBCS, mun2
13:30 GMT+1

Queens Park Rangers
1–1–5, (1–1–1 Home)

Liverpool
3–1–3, (1–0–2 Away)

YAHOO!

Right: Siri is now equipped with sports knowledge.

FACEBOOK AND TWITTER

Social-networking services, like Facebook and Twitter, are probably the most-used apps on many iPhones. You can log into your Facebook and Twitter accounts through your iPhone, upload photos, send Chat messages, update your status and browse friend and follower activity.

SYNCING FACEBOOK AND TWITTER ON YOUR iPHONE

You can log into your Facebook and Twitter accounts in the iOS settings. This enables you to share content from other apps like Photos easily, allows you to dictate status updates to Siri and to integrate Facebook events or birthdays into your calendar.

1. Head to Settings and scroll down to Facebook/Twitter.

2. Select 'Add Account' and log in with your username and password.

3. Follow the prompt to download the standalone app from the App Store.

Right: You can link up your Facebook account in the Settings app.

Posting Photos & Videos to Facebook and Twitter

The iPhone has a fantastic camera (we'll discuss this more in the next chapter), so why not share those snaps with friends and followers on social media? It's easy to share a photo directly from your iPhone.

1. Go to the Photos app and find the photo you'd like to post.

2. Hit the Share icon at the bottom of the screen and select Facebook/Twitter.

3. Type in a caption or tweet to accompany the photo and hit 'Post'.

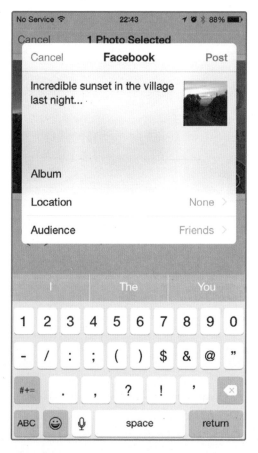

Above: It's easy to post to Facebook from your Photos app.

Configuring Facebook Notifications

Facebook notifications can be quite overwhelming at times, so you can choose what you'd like to be pushed to your iPhone using the Facebook app. For example, you may wish to be notified of Friend Requests but not Messages.

1. Open the Facebook app and hit the More tab.

2. Select Settings > Notifications.

3. Tick and untick the various notifications.

POPULAR THIRD-PARTY APPS

Third-party apps make your iPhone truly your own. These apps can often replace Apple's default solutions. We have raided the App Store to bring you our favourites, and have listed them on page 126.

Video, Music and Gaming Apps

The likes of YouTube, Netflix and Spotify allow you to stream video and music to your iPhone over the internet. There are also thousands of great touchscreen games to enjoy. Head to page 126 to see some of our picks.

Hot Tip

If you'd like to use the Facebook Chat service, you'll need to download a separate app from the App Store, called Messenger.

Above: You can configure Facebook notifications within the Facebook app.

THE FUN STUFF

CAMERA AND PHOTOGRAPHY

The iPhone has a fantastic compact camera that, on most occasions, will allow you to leave your compact snapper at home. Not only does it take great pictures and video, but there are also countless editing and sharing tools. Snap. Edit. Share. Repeat.

TAKING PICTURES AND VIDEO ON AN iPHONE

Open the Camera app on the homescreen or by swiping up on the camera icon on the lock screen. This will instantly open the camera shutter and you'll see the subject. From here, you can tap the capture button to take a picture or swipe left to open the camcorder. Anything you shoot will be saved in your Photos app and, if you're using iCloud, backed up over the web.

CAMERA SETTINGS

There's much more to taking pictures on an iPhone than just hitting the shutter button. Here are some ways to take better photos.

Left: The iOS camera interface.

Focus and Exposure

Tap anywhere on the display to ensure the lens focuses on the correct area, giving the camera a second to adjust before snapping the photo. In iOS 8, you'll see a little sun icon next to the focus square. Drag this up and down to adjust the lighting.

Flash

The default setting is Auto, which means the iPhone will make a decision about whether flash is needed. Tap the lightning bolt to turn it on and off.

Taking Selfies

Taking 'selfies' and posting them online has become very popular. Tap the camera icon in the top-right corner to switch the camera to face you.

Timer

Select the clock icon to give yourself a three- or 10-second window before the camera takes the photo.

HDR Photos

High Dynamic Range allows users to capture photos that combine low exposure and high exposures. The result should be a photo with balanced lighting.

Hot Tip

Add live photo filter effects by hitting the icon in the bottom-left corner.

Above: Tap the intended focal point of the shot on the touchscreen.

Photo Size and Shape

The default view takes a traditionally-shaped photo. Swiping right moves to Square, which is handy for a photo that's going to be uploaded to Instagram. Swiping right again opens the Pano (panoramic) setting.

Below: You can take sweeping panoramas using your iPhone.

Above: The front-facing iPhone camera is perfect for taking 'selfies'.

Taking Panoramas

You can capture a sweeping landscape or a massive family photo with the Pano setting. This requires little more than a steady hand.

1. Swipe right twice within the camera interface to get to Pano.

2. Line up your shot and press the capture button.

3. Now slowly and steadily move the phone to the right until you've captured the entire shot and hit capture again.

The process can take a few tries to perfect. If at first you don't succeed....

SHOOTING VIDEO

Swiping left in the camera menu unlocks the camcorder, where you can record full HD video, super slow-motion video (iPhone 5S and up) and, in iOS 8, Time Lapse videos, which can be sped up to show several minutes of footage in just a few seconds.

Hot Tip

Mac users can easily import their photos to their computer using iPhoto.

Hot Tip

To snap a photo of whatever is on your iPhone's screen, press the home button and the sleep/wake button together. The screenshot will appear in the Photos app.

Above: The newer iPhones are able to take super slow-motion video.

EDITING AND SHARING PHOTOS/VIDEO

Even the most masterful photos can sometimes require a little touching up before they go public. On the iPhone, it can be done with just a couple of taps on the screen, allowing users to share beautiful photos with friends.

EDITING PHOTOS

Once captured, a photo is saved to the Photos app. You can tap the last photo thumbnail on the capture screen to go straight to it. Hit 'Edit' to enter the editing menu.

- **Auto-Enhance:** Tap the magic wand to magically adjust the colours and lighting in your photo. It doesn't always work, but in many cases, it's a quick fix.

- **Crop:** Cut out unwanted elements of a photo by dragging the crop tool in and out.

- **Filter:** Add a filter to give the photo a different look and feel. Have a play.

Left: You can straighten out images with the crop tool.

○ **Colour and lighting**: Select 'Light', 'Colour' or 'B&W' to adjust the intensity of the effect by sliding left and right.

Editing Video

To trim your video clip to the perfect length, enter the clip in the Photos app and drag the arrows at the edges of the filmstrip in and out. Select 'Trim' when complete.

Other Shooting and Editing Apps

The Apple editing solution is quite basic, but there are plenty more powerful editing tools out there, such as Camera + and Photoshop Touch.

Hot Tip

Pressing and holding the video timeline will stretch out the section, allowing extra-fine editing.

Above: Dragging in the timeline indicators allows you to trim video clips.

SHARING PHOTOS

Sharing a photo you're proud of can be really rewarding, and the iPhone makes that process very simple. As with webpages in Safari and many other apps, select the Share icon to choose the destination for your photo (Facebook, Twitter, Message, Email, etc.) from the list.

Hot Tip

To share multiple photos in one message/email/post, hit 'Select' in the photos app and tap each photo you want to send.

Above: You can share iPhone photos via multiple core apps.

Instagram

One of the most popular photo-sharing tools out there, Instagram allows users to crop and add filters and effects to their photos to give them a retro, Polaroid-style feel. It's free to download from the App Store. It also allows you to upload 15-second video clips.

Hot Tip

If you have an Apple AirPrint-enabled printer, you can print photos, documents, emails and more.

Flickr and Vimeo

Like Twitter and Facebook, you can log into a Flickr (photo-sharing) and Vimeo (video-sharing) account through the Settings > General menu. This allows you to upload snaps or clips directly from the Photos app.

Above: Instagram is one of the most popular photo-sharing apps. You can also follow your favourite celebrities' posts.

iCloud Photo Sharing

This allows you to share photos with exactly the people you want, rather than everyone on your Facebook page. You can invite friends and set up groups to which other people can contribute.

1. Select the photo(s) you wish to share and choose 'iCloud Photo Sharing'.

2. Choose 'New Shared Album' and give it a name.

3. Choose your recipients, add a comment and select 'Post'.

4. The album will appear in the Shared section of the Photos app.

Below: iCloud Photo Sharing is great for sharing snaps with groups of friends and family.

Hot Tip

To save a photo as your wallpaper or assign it to a contact, press the Share button and swipe through the options.

MUSIC AND VIDEO

The iPhone is a great portable multimedia player and handheld games console. You can add, download or stream music and video, while also loading your phone with fun and immersive games. Commuting will never be the same again.

THE iTUNES STORE

Here, you can buy and download music, TV shows and movies and rent the latest blockbuster releases. Everything is added directly to your phone.

Purchasing from the iTunes Store

1. Open the iTunes Store App.

2. Browse the Music, Movies and TV Shows tabs or hit 'Search' to find a specific title.

3. After finding the stuff you'd like to download, tap 'Buy'.

4. Enter your Apple ID password to confirm the purchase.

Right: Your favourite albums are all available to download from the iTunes Store.

Hot Tip

You have 30 days to watch iTunes movie rentals, but once you start watching, you must finish it within 24 hours.

Below: You can also rent or buy movies from iTunes.

5. The item will begin downloading. When complete, it will be available in the Music or Video app.

Transferring Your Media to the iPhone

Many folks have a computer loaded with iTunes music and video. You can easily transfer this content to your iPhone.

1. Plug the iPhone into your computer via the charging (USB) cable.

2. iTunes should load automatically and begin backing up your phone.

3. Tap the iPhone button in the top-right of the program.

4. Toggle the Sync settings in the Summary and Media headings.

5. Press Sync.

Restoring Purchases

Previous iTunes purchases can be downloaded to any device associated with an Apple ID. So, if you've bought an album on your iPhone, you can easily get it on your iPad.

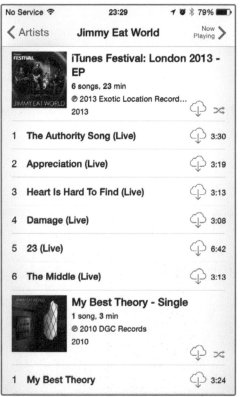

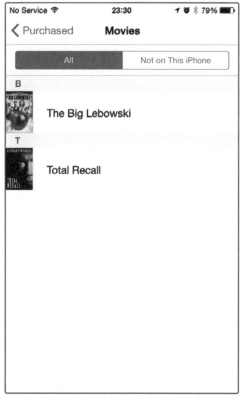

Above: Any media you've ever purchased with your Apple ID is stored by iCloud.

Above: Movies you've purchased are also available at any time through iCloud.

1. Head to iTunes Store > More > Purchases to download via iCloud.

2. You can also set purchases to download automatically to other devices. Go to Settings > iTunes and App Store and configure Automatic Downloads.

iTunes Family Sharing

A new feature in iOS 8, Family Sharing allows users to share music, movies, apps, photos and more with up to six family members. So, if you purchase a movie through one Apple ID, you can link it to other members of the household so they can see it too.

PLAYING MUSIC AND MOVIES

Now the content is loaded on to the iPhone, we can actually get on with enjoying it. Simply tap the Music or Video apps and scroll through to select what you want to hear or watch.

Listening to Music

The Now Playing screen shows album artwork and also allows you to pause, skip and adjust volume. You can also toggle the Shuffle or Repeat settings with a single tap.

Watching Video

Your video files are, as you'd expect, stored in the Video app. After you've made your selection, you'll be taken to the playback interface, where you can play, pause, rewind and fast-forward.

Right: The Music app's Now Playing interface.

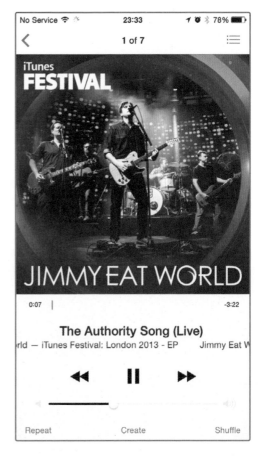

STREAMING MEDIA

Storing all of those music and video files on your phone can take up most of its memory. However, there are plenty of apps that allow you to access great content by streaming it over your phone's internet connection. Some of our favourites are listed on page 126.

Hot Tip

To access media controls easily while the phone is locked, simply tap the home button to pause, skip, and alter the volume.

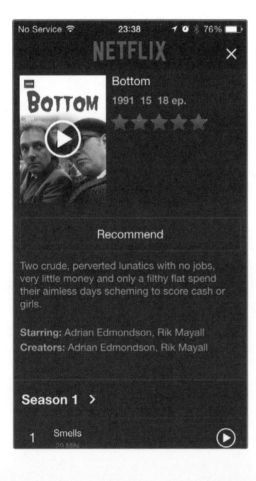

Above: Netflix offers thousands of movies and TV shows over the internet.

GAMING

The iPhone is actually one of the most popular gaming devices in the world. With fast processors, advanced graphics technology and a brilliant and responsive touchscreen, it has opened the door to a new era of gaming.

Above: Classic board games, like Scrabble, can be played on a touchscreen too.

DOWNLOADING GAMES FOR YOUR iPHONE

As with apps discussed in the previous chapter, games can be downloaded from the App Store. Open it up and hit 'Categories' and press 'Games' to go directly to the library. Download to your heart's content!

Great iPhone Games

There are almost too many to mention, but head to page 126 for a selection of titles that encompass a wide range of styles, genres and control methods.

BOOKS AND MAGAZINES

You can download books directly to your iPhone via the iBooks Store, anything from the latest bestsellers to free, out-of-print classics. You can download them in the same way you would an app from the App Store. Your purchases and free downloads are remembered by iCloud and made available on your other devices.

Reading a Book

1. Tap the book to open it from the last read page. If you're reading it for the first time, it'll open from the beginning.

2. To turn pages, swipe from right to left.

3. Select the list to access contents and bookmarks.

4. Hit the 'aA' icon to alter text size, brightness, fonts, colours, etc. If you want to scroll rather than turn pages, turn on the scrolling view.

Hot Tip
If you already own or have owned an Amazon Kindle reader, you can import your library to your iPhone via the free-to-download Kindle app.

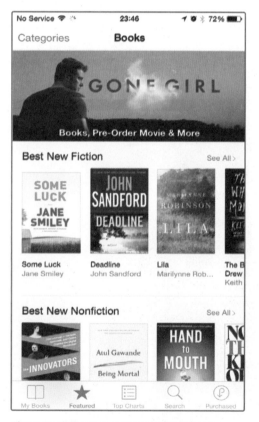

Above: The iBooks store is awash with the latest bestsellers.

TECHNICAL & TROUBLESHOOTING

MEMORY

There are only so many apps, films, videos and photos you can fit on an iPhone. As we have mentioned before, iPhones come in anything from 16 GB to 128 GB editions.

No Service 🔘	00:10	🕐 🔘 ✳ 65% 🔋
‹ Usage	**Storage**	

STORAGE

🌸 Photos & Camera	9.4 GB	›
🟢 Spotify	1.5 GB	›
💬 Messages	966 MB	›
🎸 GarageBand	722 MB	›
⭐ iMovie	664 MB	›
🖥 Keynote	532 MB	›
✏️ Pages	386 MB	›
📊 Numbers	368 MB	›
e Elevate	203 MB	›
🎵 Music	186 MB	›
🐦 Twitter	180 MB	›
f Facebook	174 MB	›

MAKING SPACE ON YOUR iPHONE

In the Usage menu hit 'Manage Storage'. This will tell you which apps are occupying the space. The worst offenders are usually media files, like music, videos, photos and games.

- **Games**: Maybe you could sacrifice any games you don't play any more?

- **iTunes Movies**: Dump big media files and re-add them at your leisure.

- **Music**: Switch to an internet music-streaming app like Spotify, which doesn't store music.

- **Photos**: Back photos up via iCloud or Dropbox and then delete them from the phone to free up space.

Left: Check out which apps are taking up a lot of storage space.

BATTERY

If you can get a day's usage out of your iPhone without recharging, you're doing well, but there are plenty of steps you can take to eke more life out of your mobile device.

PRESERVING BATTERY LIFE

There are several steps you can take to make your battery last a little longer.

1. Decrease the screen brightness (*see* page 25).

2. Switch from 4G back to 3G mobile data (Settings > Cellular and turn off Enable 4G).

3. Turn off Bluetooth and Wi-Fi, if you can spare it.

4. Change the frequency the iPhone searches for email (Settings > Mail, Contacts, Calendars > Fetch New Data and turn off Push data).

Right: The Battery Usage menu identifies which apps have been consuming the most juice.

No Service 🕙	00:11	🕙 64%
‹ Usage	**Battery Usage**	

TIME SINCE LAST FULL CHARGE

Usage	2 Hours, 30 Minutes
Standby	2 Hours, 50 Minutes

BATTERY USAGE

Last 24 Hours	Last 7 Days

	Home & Lock Screen	26%
	Spotify
Audio	17%
	Hangouts
Background Activity	10%
	Photos	6%
	No Cell Coverage	5%
	Skype
Background Activity	5%
	Maps	5%
	Instagram	4%

No Service	00:12	64%

❮ General **Background App Refresh**

Background App Refresh ⬤▬

Allow apps to refresh their content when on Wi-Fi or cellular in the background. Turning off apps may help preserve battery life.

	BBC Sport	▬⚪
	Dropbox	▬⚪
	Facebook	▬⚪
	Gmail	⚪▬
	Guardian	⚪▬
	Hangouts	▬⚪
	Instagram	▬⚪
	Mailbox	▬⚪
	Messenger	▬⚪
	NFL Fantasy	⚪▬

Above: Switching off Background App Refresh can conserve battery life.

Hot Tip
Did you know you can charge your iPhone by plugging the USB cable into your computer?

5. Turn off Background App Refresh (Settings > General > Background App Refresh and turn it off).

6. Close unused apps: double-tap the home button and swipe the app cards up.

Battery Problems
If that doesn't help, there may be one buggy app that's hogging too much power. Go to Settings > General > Usage > Battery Usage and look at the percentages. Delete the worst offenders, if you can spare them.

Battery Failure
If none of this works, take the iPhone to your local Apple store. iPhone batteries have a finite life and performance will drop off after a while. The store will run a test and let you know whether a replacement is required.

TOUCH ID AND PASSCODE

When you set up your iPhone, you should have set up a four-digit passcode, and if you're using an iPhone 5S/6/6 Plus, the Touch ID fingerprint sensor. These enable you to gain access to the phone when in locked mode. If not, head to Settings and browse down to Touch ID & Passcode (just 'Passcode' on older phones).

MULTIPLE FINGERPRINTS (iPHONE 5s/6/6 PLUS ONLY)

You can add more digits to your Touch ID fingerprint sensor. This is useful if picking up the phone with your other hand, or if you share an iPhone with a family member.

1. Head to Settings > Touch ID & Passcode.

2. Enter your four-digit passcode.

3. Select 'Add a Fingerprint'.

4. Follow the onscreen instructions, placing your finger repeatedly on the sensor until a complete picture of the print has been built up.

Right: Touch ID and passcode settings.

No Service · 00:16 · 63%

‹ Settings **Touch ID & Passcode**

USE TOUCH ID FOR:

iPhone Unlock

iTunes & App Store

Use your fingerprint instead of your Apple ID password when buying from the iTunes & App Store.

FINGERPRINTS

Finger 1 ›

Finger 2 ›

Add a Fingerprint…

Turn Passcode Off

Change Passcode

No Service 📶	00:17	🔋 63%

Change Passcode   Cancel

Enter your old passcode

— — — —

1	2 ABC	3 DEF
4 GHI	5 JKL	6 MNO
7 PQRS	8 TUV	9 WXYZ
	0	⊗

CHANGING A PASSCODE

Every so often, it doesn't hurt to alter the passcode used to unlock your device.

1. Enter Touch ID & Passcode settings.
2. Select 'Change Passcode'.
3. Enter the old passcode.
4. Enter a new passcode twice.
5. Remember it!

Right: To change your old passcode, you'll first need to enter the old one.

BACKING UP YOUR iPHONE

Keeping your iPhone backed up is one of the most important things you need to do and you should do it regularly. That way, if it drops into the bath, all is not lost....

BACKING UP THROUGH iTUNES

An iTunes back-up is great, because it safeguards everything on your iPhone. If, for example, your iPhone conks out, you can restore a new one from this back-up and everything can be restored to the new one.

Above: To back up via iTunes, you must sync your iPhone using your computer.

1. Plug your iPhone into the computer via the USB cable and wait for iTunes to load on your computer (get it at iTunes.com if you don't have it).

2. Select the iPhone tab in the top-right corner. The iPhone will sync with iTunes.

3. In the Summary section, head to Backups and select 'Back up to this computer'.

4. Every time you plug your iPhone in, the back-up will update with the most recent information.

Backing Up via iCloud

iCloud back-ups store only the most frequently accessed information, such as your contacts, account settings, documents and photos (via iCloud photostreams).

1. Head to Settings > iCloud > Backup.

2. Turn on 'iCloud Backup'.

If you backup via iCloud, your computer will no longer back everything up via iTunes.

Left: Backing up your iPhone to iCloud stores the most frequently accessed information.

LOST, STOLEN OR BROKEN iPHONES

While an inconvenience and unfortunate if uninsured, a lost, stolen or broken iPhone doesn't have to be the end of the world.

RESTORING AN iPHONE

When setting up your new/replacement/ existing iPhone, when prompted, select 'Restore from iCloud/iTunes Backup' and select a back-up. For the latter, the iPhone will need to be plugged into iTunes. This will restore all content to your phone, although you will have to take some additional set-up steps.

Recovery Mode

In rare circumstances, an iPhone will encounter a bug and enter 'recovery mode', which will show an iTunes logo and a charging cable on the screen. The only way to get around this is to restore the iPhone.

1. Plug the iPhone into iTunes. The Summary section will show the phone is in recovery mode.

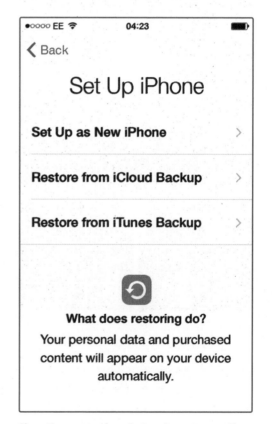

Above: You can restore from a back-up when setting up an iPhone.

Below: When this appears on your iPhone screen, it's time to restore.

2. Select 'Restore iPhone'. This will wipe all content from the phone.

3. In set-up, select 'Restore from iCloud/iTunes Backup' to return all content.

Locked Out of Your iPhone?

After a certain number of passcode attempts, your iPhone will go into lockdown. You'll need to recover your phone. Plug into iTunes, back up and then restore.

FIND MY iPHONE

Find My iPhone allows you to track the last-known location of your iPhone. This can be important if it's stolen, or simply mislaid. It also allows you to lock and erase the device remotely. Enable it by going to Settings > iCloud > Find My iPhone. Here's what to do if you lose your phone:

1. Head to iCloud.com on the web and log into
    your account. Select 'Find My iPhone'. You
    can pinpoint it on a map, which is good if,
    for example, you left it at home.

2. If it's in the same location as you, you can make
    the phone ring, allowing you to find it. If it's been
    stolen, you can enter Lost Mode to lock
    down the handset.

Hot Tip

**If your battery is about
to die, Find My iPhone
will send out its last-
known location.**

3. You can also erase the phone completely if you're worried a thief will access your data.

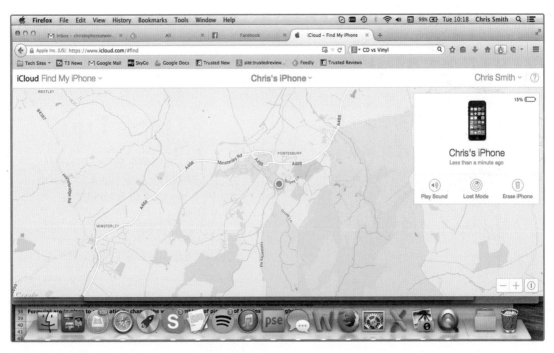

Above: Log in at iCloud.com on a web browser to access Find My iPhone.

iOS UPDATES

Apple publishes one major software update every year, but often there'll be mid-year updates to fix bugs and add new features.

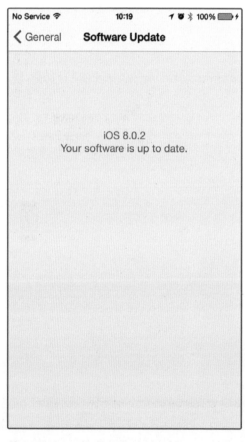

Above: It's always advisable to download the latest version of your operating system.

HOW TO UPDATE YOUR iPHONE

You should receive an alert when the software update becomes available. You can check for updates at Settings > General > Software Update. If an update is available, you can download and install when connected to Wi-Fi and have sufficient battery life.

Hot Tip

Do your apps keep crashing? Check the App Store to see if an update is available.

Can I Update My Phone?

If you have an iPhone 4S and up, you can update to iOS 8. Be warned though, if it's an older phone, it may perform less efficiently on the newest software. If you're unsure, you may want to stick to iOS 7.

CONNECTIVITY ISSUES

If you're experiencing signal loss, lack of internet connectivity, no mobile data or Wi-Fi problems, they're often environmental issues, but sometimes there's a quick fix.

A Jolt to the System?

There are several ways you can give your iPhone a quick jolt if things aren't working as you'd like.

- **Enter and exit Airplane Mode in the Control Center**: Tap the plane, give it a few seconds and tap again.

- **Wi-Fi/Cellular data**: Turn them on and off in the corresponding menus in Settings.

- **Restart**: Hold down the iPhone's home and power buttons at the same time to give your iPhone a fresh start.

Hot Tip

Not enough memory to update the software via Wi-Fi? Plug into iTunes and do it through your computer.

Above: Placing the phone in Airplane Mode shuts off all internet, mobile and Bluetooth connectivity.

USEFUL APPS

POPULAR THIRD-PARTY APPS

Third-party apps make your iPhone truly your own. These apps can often replace Apple's default solutions.

Amazon: If you love to do your shopping online, there are countless app versions of popular websites. Amazon's is a great example.

BBC News: The App Store is loaded with app versions of popular websites and news sources. These self-contained programs mean you don't have to browse to the website in Safari. Some, like BBC News, also offer notifications of breaking news.

Endomondo: The iPhone's motion sensors and GPS technology make it a great fitness aid. Endomondo allows you to track your runs, bike rides and walks. It also works nicely with Apple's Health app.

Google Maps: Up until iOS 6, Google Maps powered the mapping experience. Now Apple has its own app, but many users still prefer Google's free app.

Shazam: This genius app is one of the most popular on the App Store. Don't know the name or artist for a song on the radio? Let Shazam listen for an answer in seconds.

Skype: Offering a combination of Messages and FaceTime features, Skype is one of the most popular communication apps out there. It's free to download and join, and lets you send messages and engage in voice and video calls for free over an internet connection.

WhatsApp: A messaging platform that allows you to share texts, pictures, videos and more with friends or groups. Handy if you have lots of friends on different mobile platforms.

Yelp: Maps apps can be good for finding a restaurant or point of interest, but Yelp excels at it. It'll show nearby amenities, contact details, menus, directions and user reviews submitted by its giant community.

STREAMING MEDIA

Access great content by streaming it over your phone's internet connection.

BBC iPlayer: This allows users to watch their favourite shows at their leisure, either by streaming over their internet connection or downloading for offline viewing.

Netflix: Netflix gives users the chance to watch thousands upon thousands of movies and TV shows on multiple devices. Subscriptions start from £6.99 a month.

Spotify: This app gives you 10 hours of free streaming each month, while Spotify Premium subscribers (£9.99 a month) get unlimited ad-free streaming and the opportunity to download music for offline listening.

YouTube: The everyman's video service features everything from funny cat videos that have gone viral to the latest music videos and movie trailers.

GREAT iPHONE GAMES

There are almost too many to mention, but these titles encompass a wide range of styles, genres and control methods.

Angry Birds: Surely you know this one? Use the touchscreen to pull back and position the slingshot and release to fire the Angry Bird at the egg-stealing pigs.

Asphalt 8: The iPhone has multiple movement sensors and they're great for driving games. Tilt the phone in order to steer the car, accelerate and brake.

FIFA 15: This popular football game offers a more traditional control method, with a virtual onscreen control pad. Tap buttons to pass, shoot, tackle, etc.

Fruit Ninja: Swipe the screen furiously in order to slice the fruit items, but watch out for the bombs.

Scrabble: The App Store is packed with traditional board games, optimized for touchscreen play.

The Simpsons: Tapped Out: Springfield has been destroyed by a nuclear accident. This role-playing game allows you to rebuild it to your own design, Kwik-E-Mart and all.

Temple Run: An example of the 'endless run' genre, you swipe in different directions to avoid obstacles and certain death.

INDEX